Berger + Parkkinen
Die Botschaften
der Nordischen Länder
Berlin

Text
Klaus-Dieter Weiß

Photographien / Photographs
Christian Richters

Edition Axel Menges

Herausgeber/Editor: Axel Menges

© 2006 Edition Axel Menges, Stuttgart/London
ISBN 3-930698-40-4

Zweite, unveränderte Auflage
Second, unrevised edition

Reproduktionen/Reproductions: Bild & Text Joachim
Baun, Fellbach
Druck und Bindearbeiten/Printing and binding:
Everbest Printing Co., Ltd., China

Übersetzung ins Englische/Translation into English:
Michael Robinson
Design: Axel Menges

Inhalt

Contents

Klaus-Dieter Weiß
Politik in Bildern – die Botschaften der Nordischen Länder in Berlin

Berlin ist interessant, wild und rauh – nach der Einwohnerzahl aber nicht einmal halb so groß wie Paris, London oder New York. Begünstigt durch riesige Brachflächen im Zentrum, entwickelte die Stadt nach dem Fall der Mauer uralte Stadtqualitäten. Aber auch darin zeigt sich nicht nur Vergangenheit, sondern bei näherem Hinsehen Veränderung und Neubeginn. In Berlin ist man mit der Geschichte immer ruppig umgegangen.[1] Man löste die Frage der baulichen Tradition durch Abriß, auch im Fall der markantesten städtebaulichen Struktur: der Berliner Mauer. Berlin, im Vergleich zu Paris, London, Wien oder Rom der Benjamin unter den großen europäischen Metropolen, dokumentiert nach kaum mehr als 500 Jahren ganzheitlicher Entwicklung nicht Einheit, sondern Kontraste, auch in Form widerstreitender Städtebau- und Architekturideologien. Die Spannung der Stadt liegt in den Gegensätzen, in den »Kämpfen« und Auseinandersetzungen, die das Stadtbild prägen. Gerade das ist der besondere Charakter, heute aber auch die Chance dieser Stadt. Die Zerstörung von etwa 50 000 Gebäuden im Zweiten Weltkrieg und die dramatische Teilung der Stadt im Jahr 1961 sind noch heute prägend.

Neben vielfach gebrochenen Entwicklungslinien und explodierenden demographischen Daten waren für Berlin jenseits der Nazi-Diktatur immer Toleranz und Offenheit kennzeichnend, ohne die der Anspruch Weltstadt und Metropole nicht zu denken war und ist. Darum verwundert die ausgeprägte Voreingenommenheit und Skepsis, mit der gerade die britische Presse, etwa die linksliberale Tageszeitung *The Guardian,* der neuen Hauptstadt in Siegerpose begegnet: Berlin, eine Stadt angeblich, in der »die Geschichte aus jeder Pore hervorquillt, wo sich in jeder Spalte im Pflaster Monster verbergen«.[2] »Außer sporenklingenden Militärparaden, dem Anzetteln von aggressiven Kriegen und homosexuellem Kabarett hat Berlin der Welt wenig gegeben.«[3] Verständlich, daß unter diesem Blickwinkel nur die von Briten entworfenen Bauten »aufregend und überzeugend« sind.[4] So bleibt für die Botschaften der Nordischen Länder nur die Rolle eines merkwürdigen »smaragdgrünen Gürteltiers«; selbst die urbanen Achsen unter dem hermetischen Panzer zwischen den »kahlen, ausdruckslosen Einzelgebäuden« gelten als »finster« im Sinne de Chiricos.[5]

Architektonisch zeigt Berlin traditionell Härte, eine nüchterne und unsentimentale Einstellung gegenüber allem Gebauten, die Nutzwert immer über architektonische Raffinesse stellte. Der antistädtischen Stadtlandschaft Scharouns nach dem Zweiten Weltkrieg und der punktuellen Stadtreparatur der Postmoderne folgte nach der Wiedervereinigung der schwierige und umstrittene Aufbruch zur »kritischen Rekonstruktion« des historischen Zentrums, zur Rekonstruktion der nationalen Mitte. Immer noch gilt, was Ernst Bloch formulierte: »In Berlin ist mutatis mutandis immer Gründerzeit.« In

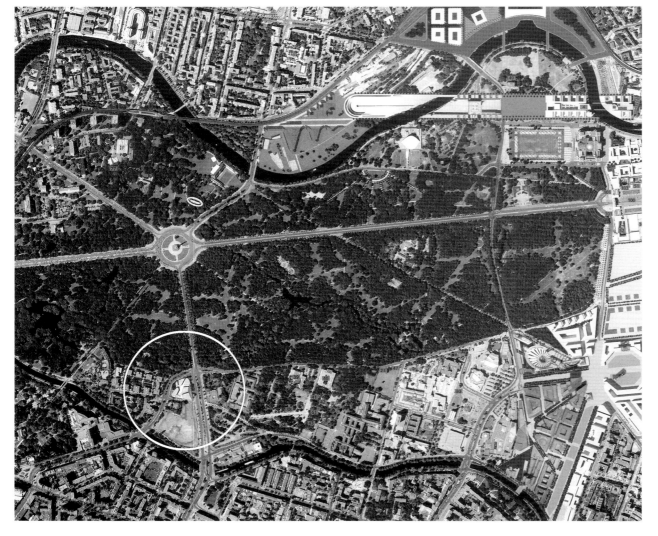

1. Luftaufnahme des Tiergartens in Berlin mit eingesetztem Modell der Botschaften der Nordischen Länder. (BSF GmbH, Diepensee, 1994; vervielfältigt mit Erlaubnis der Senatsverwaltung für Bauen, Wohnen und Verkehr, V, Berlin, vom 11. September 1998.)

1. Aerial view of the Tiergarten in Berlin with a model of the Embassies of the Nordic Countries inserted. (BSF GmbH, Diepensee, 1994; reproduced by permission of the Senatsverwaltung für Bauen, Wohnen und Verkehr, V, Berlin, from 11 September 1998.)

Klaus-Dieter Weiß
Politics in images – the Embassies of the Nordic Countries in Berlin

Berlin is interesting, untamed and rough – but not even half the size of Paris, London or New York by number of inhabitants. After the fall of the Wall, the city developed ancient urban qualities, a process that was helped by the large areas of waste land in the centre. But here too it is not just demonstrating the past: on closer examination change can be discerned, and signs of a fresh start. Berlin has always dealt roughly with history.[1] The problem of architectural tradition was solved by pulling things down, even in the case of that most striking of urban structures, the Berlin Wall. Berlin, compared with Paris, London, Vienna or Rome, is very much the youngster among the great European cities. After scarcely more than 500 years of development as an entity it does not give a sense of unity, but of contrast, in the form of urban development clashes, and of architectural ideology as well. The city's excitement lies in its contrasts, in the »fights« and conflicts that shape its image. Precisely this gives the city its special character, and also presents it with a unique opportunity. About 50 000 buildings were destroyed in the Second World War, and the city was dramatically divided in 1961; both these factors still influence the shape of the city today.

Alongside lines of development that were very frequently broken off and exploding demographic data, Berlin has always shown openness and tolerance before and after the Nazi dictatorship, both qualities being essential for any city aspiring to world status. It is therefore surprising to see the degree of prejudice and scepticism with which the British press has confronted the new capital, striking a victor's pose. Take *The Guardian*, for example: Berlin is apparently a city »that leaks history out of every pore, where every crack in the pavement conceals monsters«.[2] »Berlin has given the world little except spur-clashing military parades, the waging of aggressive war and homosexual cabaret.«[3] It is understandable that from this point of view only the buildings designed by Britons are »adventurous and convincing«.[4] So the only role left for the Embassies of the Nordic Countries is that of a remarkable »emerald armadillo«; even the urban axes under the hermetic armour between the »blank and inexpressive individual buildings« are considered »sinister« in the spirit of de Chirico.[5]

Architecturally speaking, Berlin is traditionally hard, treating everything that is built soberly and unsentimentally, and always valuing functionality more highly than architectural refinement. Scharoun's anti-city cityscape after the Second World War and Post-Modernism's isolated stabs at urban repair was followed after reunification by the difficult and controversial start made on »critical reconstruction« of the historical centre, the reconstruction of the centre of the nation. Ernst Bloch's formulation is still true: »Berlin is still stuck in the late 19th century, mutatis mutandis.« Berlin above all cities is the one where people now hugely enjoy poking about in the ashes of architectural ideas that have long since died out in order to draw on arbitrary historical modes for creating buildings (Michael Mönninger). It also still has the continuing allure of a possible new Stadtschloss, but despite all the urban and architectural blandness of the newly created traditions, despite

all the scepticism with which the British press can say that »Berlin is on the march again«,[6] we have still seen an accumulation of »little slips« running counter to all this, like Zvi Hecker's Heinz Galinski School in 1995 (German Critics' Prize for Architecture), Daniel Libeskind's Jewish Museum in 1999 (German Prize for Architecture) and finally in October 1999 the Embassies of the Nordic Countries by Alfred Berger and Tiina Parkkinen.

Have the architecture and symbolism of the Informel changed with the world currency of its originators? Does Berlin of all places embody a different and more open republic from Bonn? »Big-mouthed claims of becoming a metropolis in the eyes of the whole world, or achieving the glitter of the golden (and socially wretched) twenties, which outdid Paris – these are things that cannot be either decided or bought with money. Berlin will develop something that Bonn could not manage over the past fifty years, sometimes lamented with an eye on its neighbours: the attractive qualities of a national centre.« This reticent and frank vision by Egon Bahr outlines a realistic and potentially successful view that seems to fit more accurately with the »heroic« modesty of the Embassies of the Nordic Countries that it would with recreating the Schloss or other major buildings that have disappeared.

Four sharp-edged street-gorges, electrified in their perspective and tumbling over each other like spillikins, carve up an urban block to form a complex, amorphous structure on the city side. The Nordic countries are second to none in popular terms in their high aesthetic claims, and are far superior to Europe as a community of states expressed symbolically in architectural terms. Not even the 16 federal German states managed to create a look for themselves that was similarly all-embracing and yet individual. The stubbornness of the individual state offices in Berlin cost millions and millions and a great deal of superfluous organizational effort, and yet in the end they still ended up bundled together in the Bundesrat. The Austro-Finnish team of Alfred Berger and Tiina Parkkinen have successfully brought off a coup that gives politics an enticing image: far from particularism and princely splendour that have long been a thing of the past.

Early in the last, the twentieth, century the architects of the Neues Bauen – New Building – movement were looking for a vision of a new society. Architecture was highly significant in symbolic terms at the time of rebuilding after the First World War. Instead of building the unique war memorials of a »peace state« as a monument to constructive social forces, 1918 unleashed storms of enthusiasm: architecture as a »crystalline expression of men's most noble thoughts, their fervour, their humanity, their faith, their religion« (Walter Gropius, 1919). Bruno Taut in the same year: »It is unthinkable that millions of people should fall prey completely to materialism, just carry on living, without knowing what they are there for. Something must live in every man's breast that lifts him above the temporal and that makes him feel a sense of community with his fellow men, his nation and the whole world.«

On the same level, Günter Behnisch, writing in 1992, called for a moral basis for democracy, quite separate from all formal, technical, practical and functional and administrative connections.[7] Here he was referring to an essay by the international lawyer and politician Carlo Schmid, who died in 1979: »The technique of demo-

Berlin, ausgerechnet in der Stadt, in der man heute so gern in der Asche längst erloschener Baugedanken herumstochert, um sich auf willkürlich konstruierte Schöpfungsordnungen aus der Geschichte zu berufen (Michael Mönninger), samt eines immer wieder neu lockenden Stadtschlosses, häufen sich bei allem städtebaulichen und architektonischen Gleichmaß der neu geschaffenen Traditionen, bei aller Skepsis der englischen Presse vor einem »Berlin marschiert wieder«[6] die »Betriebsunfälle« – so die Heinz-Galinski-Schule von Zvi Hecker 1995 (Deutscher Kritikerpreis für Architektur), das Jüdische Museum von Daniel Libeskind 1999 (Deutscher Architekturpreis) und schließlich im Oktober 1999 die Botschaften der Nordischen Länder von Alfred Berger und Tiina Parkkinen.

Haben sich Architektur und Symbolik des Informellen mit der Weltläufigkeit ihrer Urheber gewandelt? Verkörpert ausgerechnet Berlin eine andere, offenere Republik als Bonn? »Großmäulige Ansprüche, Metropole mit Weltgeltung zu werden oder den Glanz der goldenen (und gesellschaftlich elenden) zwanziger Jahre wieder erreichen zu wollen, der Paris überstrahlte – so etwas kann man weder beschließen noch mit Geld kaufen. Berlin wird entwickeln, was Bonn nicht leisten konnte in den zurückliegenden fünfzig Jahren, mit dem Blick auf die Nachbarn zuweilen beklagt: die Attraktivität einer nationalen Mitte.« Mit dieser zurückhaltenden und offenen Vision Egon Bahrs ist eine realistische und erfolgversprechende Perspektive umrissen, der die

»heroische« Bescheidenheit der Botschaften der Nordischen Länder mehr zu entsprechen scheint als die Neuinszenierung untergegangener Schlösser und Akademien.

Vier wie Mikadostäbe übereinanderfallende, perspektivisch elektrisierte, scharfkantige Straßenschluchten zerschneiden einen Baublock zur Stadt in einer komplexen amorphen Skulptur. Die nordischen Länder, in ihrem hohen ästhetischen Anspruch unübertroffen volkstümlich, überflügelt Europa als Staatengemeinschaft architektonisch schon in der Symbolik. Auf einen ähnlich gemeinsamen und doch individuellen Auftritt sind nicht einmal die 16 deutschen Bundesländer gekommen. Der Eigensinn der individuellen Berliner Landesvertretungen kostet stolze Millionenbeträge und viel überflüssigen Organisationsaufwand – um schließlich im Bundesrat doch gebündelt zu werden. Dem in Wien angesiedelten österreichisch-finnischen Architektenteam Alfred Berger und Tiina Parkkinen ist ein Coup gelungen, der der Politik ein Bild gibt, das Ansporn ist: fern vergangener Kleinstaaterei und Fürstenherrlichkeit.

Zu Beginn des vergangenen, des 20. Jahrhunderts suchten die Architekten des Neuen Bauens nach der Vision einer neuen Gesellschaft. In der Zeit des Wiederaufbaus nach dem Ersten Weltkrieg hatte Architektur eine große symbolische Bedeutung. Anstelle von singulären Kriegsdenkmälern eine »Friedensstadt« als Monument der konstruktiven gesellschaftlichen Kräfte

2. Berger + Parkkinen, die Botschaften der Nordischen Länder, Berlin. Ideenskizze.
3. Berger + Parkkinen, die Botschaften der Nordischen Länder. Modell.
4. Berger + Parkkinen, die Botschaften der Nordischen Länder. Luftaufnahme. (Helicolor-Luftbild-Ost GmbH.)

2. Berger + Parkkinen, the Embassies of the Nordic Countries, Berlin. Idea sketch.
3. Berger + Parkkinen, die Botschaften der Nordischen Länder. Model.
4. Berger + Parkkinen, the Embassies of the Nordic Countries, Berlin. Aerial view. (Helicolor-Luftbild-Ost GmbH.)

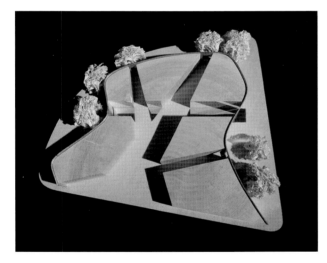

cratic procedures finds its ultimate meaning in bringing human life together within a constitution that does justice to the dignity of all and under which everyone – including minorities – are able to develop their abilities in freedom and thus find self-realization and affirmation of their nature. All that appertains to this has entered the political awareness of society as ›human rights‹, in the course of a long historical process ... democracy is an opportunity for us all to handle its instruments in such a way that human beings are always central in the state as well. It is not yet the pure vessel of humanity; but it offers us resources with the help of which we can humanize the state.« Man is central to the Embassies of the Nordic Countries, which come very close to meeting this requirement, in the image of the public square or forum. This is not architecture that invokes power, but an empty urban space, that has to be constantly refilled. In other words: not a Bastille of bureaucracy, but the street, which is necessary as a defence against the encroachment of the state.

The »forecourt« of power changed with the onset of Modernism. State power forfeited its sovereignty and no longer presented itself as a concrete body whose greatness and glory could be spectacularly presented in public streets and squares, as happened in the days of the medieval rulers or the princes of the Renaissance. State power became anonymous, invisible and functional with the growing flood of news and information that had to be compressed, processed and transformed into knowledge. The state surrounded itself with an administrative system that put the sets of data into order as they accumulated, addressed them, then committed them to archives. Power shifted from the centre to the periphery, from the glare of publicity into opaque forecourts, where ministers, advisers and secretaries do their daily work, where door follows door, corridor follows corridor, office follows office, where

clerks, messengers and couriers control the flow of information from and to the person who actually wields the power, who then himself, as the cleverest and most powerful figure of all, »is able to distil at least a few drops from this surging, infinite sea of truth and lies, realities and possibilities« (Carl Schmitt).[8] This culture of the anteroom, which is merely a culture of archivists and bureaucrats, of tables, statistics and documents, is broken up in the truest sense of the word by Alfred Berger and Tiina Parkkinen's design. The central architectural approach is not to provide a framework for bureaucracy, the basic necessities for »fillers-in of forms, note-writers, list-makers, writers-down of this and that, dispatchers, administrators, adders-up« (Martin Kieren). Berger + Parkkinen want their architecture to be openly accessible, and publicly accessible at least in feeling welcoming and manageable to the public. This approach shows the difference between this constellation of buildings, which is in six parts but entirely single-minded in its urban aims and symbolism, and the typologies proposed by the other competition entrants. Superficially the ensemble thrives on its contrasts and contradictions, on a complexity with which Berlin's new and old cityscape – sometimes aware of tradition and doggedly persistent, sometimes technocratically banal – has not been confronted for a long time. It might be easy to concede that it is easier to humanize small departments than large mammoth structures. Even so, when all is said and done this complex houses the embassy systems of five countries, including Denmark's trade delegation.

Are the official buildings of foreign states, which are perceived as extraterritorial, like inaccessible islands, part of the cultural structure of their host country? Should the exchange of opinions across a border not cease to be restricted to heads of state and government representatives alone, but shatter official em-

zu bauen, löste 1918 Begeisterungsstürme aus: Baukunst als »kristallener Ausdruck der edelsten Gedanken der Menschen, ihrer Inbrunst, ihrer Menschlichkeit, ihres Glaubens, ihrer Religion« (Walter Gropius, 1919). Bruno Taut im selben Jahr: »Es ist nicht denkbar, daß Millionen von Menschen ganz dem Materialismus verfallen, dahinleben, ohne zu wissen, wofür sie da sind. Es muß etwas in jedes Menschen Brust leben, das ihn über das Zeitliche hinaushebt und das ihn die Gemeinschaft mit seiner Mitwelt, seiner Nation, allen Menschen und der ganzen Welt fühlen läßt.«

Auf derselben Ebene forderte Günter Behnisch 1992 für das politisch verantwortete Bauen der Demokratie eine moralische Basis abseits aller formalen, technischen, praktisch-funktionalen, juristischen und administrativen Bindungen.[7] Dabei bezog er sich auf einen Text des 1979 verstorbenen Völkerrechtlers und Politikers Carlo Schmid: »Die Technik der demokratischen Prozeduren hat ihren letzten Sinn darin, das Zusammenleben der Menschen so in Verfassung zu bringen, daß der Würde aller Genüge getan wird und allen – auch Minderheiten – institutionell die Möglichkeit gegeben wird, ihr Vermögen in Freiheit entfalten und dadurch Selbstverwirklichung und Wesensbejahung finden zu können. Was hierzu gehört, ist im Laufe eines langen geschichtlichen Prozesses als ›Menschenrechte‹ in das politische Bewußtsein der Gesellschaft eingegangen. ... Demokratie ist ein Angebot an uns alle, mit ihrem Instrumentarium so umzugehen, daß der Mensch auch im Staate immer in der Mitte steht. Sie ist noch nicht das reine Gefäß der Menschlichkeit; sie bietet uns aber Mittel an, mit deren Hilfe wir den Staat vermenschlichen können.« Im Zentrum der Botschaften der Nordischen Länder, die dieser Vorgabe sehr nahe kommen, steht mit dem Bild des öffentlichen Platzes oder Forums symbolisch der Mensch, keine Macht heischende Architektur, sondern ein leerer urbaner Raum, der immer wieder neu zu füllen ist. Mit anderen Worten: keine Bastille der Bürokratie, sondern die Straße, die nötig ist, um sich gegen Übergriffe des Staates zu wehren.

Der »Vorhof« der Macht hat sich mit dem Beginn der Moderne verändert. Die staatliche Macht büßte ihre Souveränität ein und präsentierte sich nicht mehr als konkreter Körper, dessen Glanz und Glorie wie zu Zeiten der mittelalterlichen Herrscher und Renaissancefürsten auf öffentlichen Plätzen und Straßen spektakulär inszeniert werden konnte. Mit der wachsenden Flut von Nachrichten und Informationen, die komprimiert, verarbeitet und in Wissen verwandelt werden muß, wurde staatliche Macht anonym, unsichtbar und funktional. Sie umgab sich mit einem Verwaltungssystem, das die anfallenden Datensätze ordnet, adressiert und archiviert. Vom Zentrum wanderte die Macht an die Peripherie, aus dem Licht der Öffentlichkeit in die undurchschaubaren Vorhöfe, wo Minister, Referenten und Sekretäre ihre tägliche Arbeit tun, wo sich Tür an Tür, Gang an Gang, Büro an Büro reiht, wo Schreiber, Boten und Kuriere den Nachrichtenfluß vom und zum eigentlichen Machthaber regeln, der selbst als Klügster und Mächtigster »aus diesem flutenden, unendlichen Meer von Wahrheit und Lüge, Wirklichkeiten und Möglichkeiten höchstens einige Tropfen herausschöpfen kann« (Carl Schmitt).[8] Diese Kultur des Vorraums, die lediglich eine Kultur der Archivare und Bürokraten ist, der Tabellen, Statistiken und Akten, brechen Alfred Berger und Tiina Parkkinen mit ihrem Entwurf im

wahrsten Sinne des Wortes auf. Das zentrale architektonische Motiv ist nicht die Gestaltung der Bürokratie, der Notwendigkeiten für »Formularausfüller, Zettelvollschreiber, Listenersteller, Sonstwasaufschreiber, Versender, Verwalter, Rechner« (Martin Kieren), sondern die offene, zumindest in ihrer Überschaubarkeit öffentliche Zugänglichkeit der Architektur. Dieses Motiv grenzt die sechsteilige, aber in ihrer städtebaulichen Zielsetzung und Symbolik eindeutige Konstellation von der Typologie der übrigen Wettbewerbsarbeiten ab. Vordergründig lebt das Ensemble von seinen Kontrasten und Widersprüchen, einer Komplexität, die dem neuen alten Stadtbild von Berlin – einmal traditionsbewußt beharrlich, einmal technokratisch banal – lange nicht begegnet ist. Daß kleine Behörden leichter zu vermenschlichen sind als große Mammutgebilde, mag zugegeben sein. Immerhin handelt es sich bei dem Komplex jedoch um den Botschaftsapparat von fünf Ländern einschließlich der Wirtschaftsvertretung von Dänemark.

Gehören die wie unerreichbare Inseln extraterritorial verstandenen Amtsgebäude fremder Staaten zum kulturellen Gefüge ihres Gastlandes? Soll sich der grenzüberschreitende Austausch von Meinungen nicht nur auf Staatsoberhäupter und Regierungsvertreter beschränken, sondern den amtlichen Habitus einer Botschaft interkulturell sprengen? Öffentlichkeit erleben Botschaften meist in der Form des Protestes, nicht durch ein kunstsinniges oder architekturkritisches Publikum. Pomp und Größe der russischen Botschaft jenseits des Brandenburger Tores machen den Besucher klein, nicht etwa groß. Haben Botschaften also kein Publikum, das diesen Namen verdient? Die Botschaften der Nordischen Länder provozieren solche Fragen, weil sie eine gebäudetypologisch, architektonisch und politisch grundlegend neue Antwort bereithalten. Heroisch ist diese Architektur allein in ihren bescheidenen Mitteln bei großen Zielen.

Selbst die unmittelbar beteiligten Botschafter und Monarchen scheinen mitunter erst zu ahnen, welch intelligente politische Bühne, welch brillantes Image ihnen da zum Millennium von zwei jungen, vor dem europaweiten Wettbewerb mit 222 Teilnehmern nahezu unbekannten, aber umso hartnäckigeren Architekten beschert worden ist. Große Ideen sind einfach und überzeugen ohne Debatte. Andererseits schlagen Interpretationsversuche zunächst gerne fehl, weil kein Maßstab zur Hand ist. In diese Kategorie fällt auch der gegen das Konzept der Straßenschneisen und klaren Baufluchten durchgesetzte Grußbalkon des dänischen Architekten für die dänische Botschaft. Das kleine Detail erreicht das 21. Jahrhundert als historische Reminiszenz einer politischen Architektur, die die Botschaften der Nordischen Länder neu definiert haben. Es war Königin Margarethe II. von Dänemark, die als dienstälteste unter den nordischen Staatsoberhäuptern in ihrer Eröffnungsansprache das Berlin-Bild von Hans Christian Andersen zitierte: »... schnurgerade Straßen, Palast an Palast.« Zu ergänzen wäre: Berlin, die »hochgebuffte« Ansammlung von Häusern (Theodor Fontane) oder das »monumentalste Beispiel des modernen Dilettantismus in der Stadtbaukunst« (Karl Scheffler, 1910). Dem banalen Prinzip Reihung stellen Alfred Berger und Tiina Parkkinen eine kunstvoll inszenierte, dezidiert urbane, darum scharfkantige Schneidigkeit der Gesamtanlage im Inneren entgegen, die auf eine Krempe mit Wappen hätte verzichten können. Auch

5. Berger + Parkkinen, Bibliothek in Turku, 1998. Wettbewerbsentwurf.

5. Berger + Parkkinen, library in Turku, 1998. Competition design.

bassy behaviour with an intercultural approach? Embassies usually experience the public in the form of protest, not by people who are interested in art or enjoy responding critically to architecture. The size and splendour of the Russian Embassy on the other side of the Brandenburg Gate make visitors feel small, not big. So do embassies not have a public that is worthy of the name? The Embassies of the Nordic Countries provoke questions of this kind because they have a response ready that is fundamentally new in terms of building typology, architecture and politics. This architecture is heroic only in using modest means to achieve great aims.

Even the ambassadors and monarchs who are directly involved sometimes seem to be less than fully aware of the intelligence of the public stage, the brilliance of the image they have been given for the millennium by two young and almost unknown but all the more stubborn architects who were faced with competition from 222 participants in a competition with entries from all over Europe. Big ideas are simple, and convince without argument. But attempts at interpretation are prone to failure if there is nothing available to provide a clear comparison. The Danish architect insisted on a ceremonial balcony for the Danish Embassy, and this too falls into the same category, as it goes against the grain of the concept of street lines and buildings in clear rows. This little detail arrives in the 21st century as a historical reminiscence of political

architecture that has been redefined by the Embassies of the Nordic Countries. It was Queen Margarethe II of Denmark, who delivered the opening address as the oldest of the Scandinavian monarchs in terms of years on the throne, and quoted Hans Christian Andersen's image of Berlin: »dead-straight streets, palace after palace«. One could add: Berlin as a »highly-finished« collection of buildings (Theodor Fontane) or the »most monumental example of modern dilettantism in urban architecture« (Karl Scheffler, 1910). Alfred Berger and Tiina Parkkinen confront the banal principle of accumulation with an artificially staged, decidedly urban and therefore sharp-edged incisiveness for the interior of the entire complex, which could have done without a hat-brim decorated with a coat of arms. And the architecture of the Embassies of the Nordic Countries also does not seem to be »landscaped« through and through, nor does the apparently dimensionless copper band, its 4000 individual slats supplied with their patina already formed, follow the image of the Wall as a negative gesture. The slats' fixed flutter of the eyelashes towards the Tiergarten, which can also be experienced in the interior beyond the streets and waterways, is far too marked for this to be the case. The big architectural idea of the complex as a whole is also not limited to the transparency of slats, a theme that is the subject of variations in the façades of all the embassies with the exception of the little building for Iceland, but that should be understood more as a set of layers aiming at

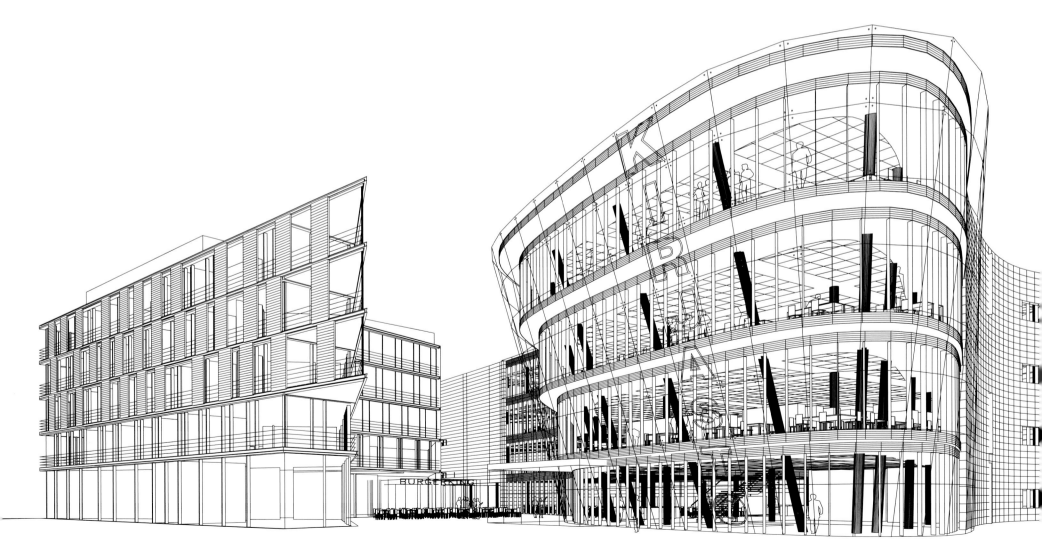

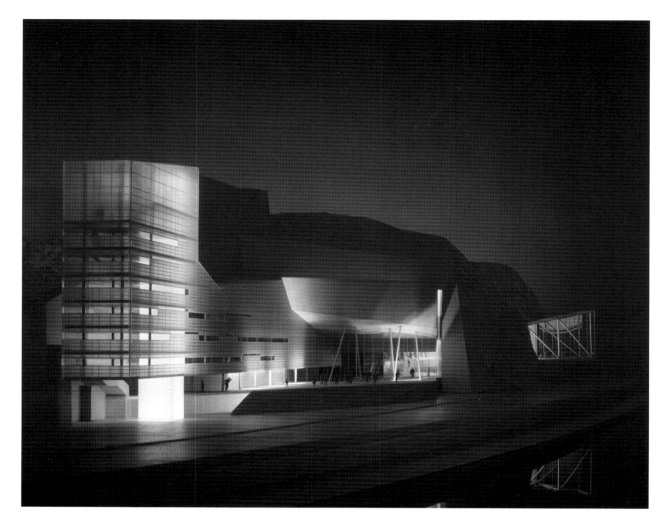

scheint die Architektur der Botschaften der Nordischen Länder weder durch und durch »landschaftlich« thematisiert, noch folgt das in 4000 Einzellamellen vorpatinierte, scheinbar dimensionslose Kupferband dem Bild der »Mauer« als abweisende Geste. Dazu spielt der fixierte Wimpernschlag der Lamellen in Richtung Tiergarten, der über die Straßen und Wasserläufe hinweg auch im Inneren zu erleben ist, eine zu große Rolle. Die große architektonische Idee der Gesamtanlage beschränkt sich andererseits nicht auf die Transparenz von Lamellen, ein Thema, das bis auf das kleine Haus Islands zwar in den Fassaden aller Botschaften variiert wird, das aber eher als Schichtung zu Vielfalt und Komplexität, denn als variable bzw. autonome Grenzbestimmung zu begreifen ist.

Was steckt hinter dieser grandiosen Synthese von fünf Ländern, sechs Gebäuden und sechs Architektenteams, die in der zweiten Stufe in jeweils eigenen, nationalen Wettbewerbsverfahren ausgewählt wurden? Die Vision, die auf der Ebene von Architektur und Design schon Realität ist, gilt der Vereinigung von Einzelinteressen zu einem größeren Ganzen – das uralte demokratische Ideal, das vielleicht nie zu einer anschaulicheren und überzeugenderen Geste gefunden hat als in diesem gegen den Berliner Tiergarten gestellten Wechselspiel von Stadt und Landschaft. Kubisch-kantige, technisch-blasse »reine« Formen kollidieren bei Berger + Parkkinen mit geometrisch »unreinen«, gebrochenen und gekurvten farbigen Formen. Dieser eher stadträumliche als architektonische Ansatz ist Ergebnis einer langwierigen Suche nach dem eigenen Selbstverständnis. Der Entwurf für eine Bibliothek in Turku

(1998), der Wettbewerbsbeitrag für das Musiktheater in Linz (1998) und ein leider im Wettbewerb ebenfalls gescheiterter, komplexer Beitrag für das Justizzentrum in Leoben (2000) sind wichtige Stationen eines eigenständigen Weges, der mit der Gründung des Büros Berger + Parkkinen im Jahr 1995 und dem Wettbewerb für die Botschaften der Nordischen Länder begann. In Berlin verkörpert das Kupferband in seiner Materialität und seiner schwungvollen Dynamik die Komponente Natur oder das Gegenbild der Rationalität. Was man zunächst nicht ahnt: Auch die regelhafte Ordnung der Kupferlamellen wird in der Kurvatur des Gebäudes durchbrochen. Abhängig von der Krümmung schwanken die Elementbreiten in fünf Dimensionen zwischen 90 und 180 cm.

Das Motiv erinnert unwillkürlich an die finnischen Seenlandschaften, die schon Alvar Aalto zu weichen, kurvigen und organischen Formen inspirierten: 1930 erstmals zur wellenförmigen Decke im Vortragssaal der Bibliothek in Viipuri, später zu Vasen, Türgriffen, Leuchten, Möbeln und dreidimensional bewegten Raumgrenzen. Ein Bild, das sich im Inneren der dänischen Botschaft und in der »Wolke« des im Atrium schwebenden finnischen Konferenzsaals wiederfindet. Ein Bild, das der Gefahr der Überrationalisierung trotzen will, der Bedrohung durch die politische, technische, ökonomische Planung, die auf der Suche nach leicht erreichbaren Zielen tief verankerte kulturelle und sinnliche Werte opfert. Die große Resonanz, die die Botschaften der Nordischen Länder in Berlin, aber auch weltweit gefunden haben, hat hier ihren Ursprung. Die rätselhafte, unberechenbare, tausendfach gebrochene, in ihren aus den

6. Berger + Parkkinen, Musiktheater in Linz, 1998. Wettbewerbsentwurf. (Photo: Gerald Zugmann.)
7. Berger + Parkkinen, Justizzentrum in Leoben, Österreich, 2000. Wettbewerbsentwurf.

6. Berger + Parkkinen, musical theatre in Linz, 1998. Competition design. (Photo: Gerald Zugmann.)
7. Berger + Parkkinen, justice centre in Leoben, Austria, 2000. Competition design.

diversity and complexity than a variable or autonomous definition of borders.

What lies behind this grandiose synthesis of five countries, six buildings and six teams of architects, selected in the second phase by their own national competitions? The vision, which is already reality on the plane of architecture and design, is concerned with fusing individual interests into a greater whole – the ancient democratic ideal that has perhaps never found a more vivid and convincing gesture than in this interplay of city and landscape that has been juxtaposed with the Tiergarten in Berlin. In Berger + Parkkinen's work,

cubic and angular, technical and pallid »pure« forms collide with geometrically »impure«, broken and curved coloured forms. This approach, which is conceived more in terms of urban space than of architecture, is the result of a long search for self-understanding. The design for a library in Turku (1998), the competition entry for a musical theatre in Linz (1998) and a complex entry for the justice centre in Leoben (2000), which unfortunately also failed in the competition, are important staging points on an independent route that started in 1995 with the foundation of the Berger + Parkkinen office and the competition for the Embassies of the Nor-

Naturkräften folgenden Farbdetails an keiner Stelle identische, noch dazu »grüne«, vor altem und neuem Baumbestand zurückweichende Fassade, die die einzelnen Botschaften zur Einheit führt, indem sie die Kurve der Stülerstraße aufgreift, dokumentiert eine Philosophie, kein Gebäude. Das Bild der das Individuum dominierenden, sterilen Stadt weicht einer Symbolik, dem Selbstverständnis der nordischen Länder, die viel enger verbunden sind als weithin bekannt.

Der Machtanspruch, den politische Architektur in der Regel etablieren möchte, kollidiert hier sichtbar mit einer langen demokratischen Tradition, dem Ziel der Gleichberechtigung, dem Stellenwert von Natur und Umwelt, dem Eintreten für Natur- und Menschenrechte. Die Botschaften der Nordischen Länder warnen damit plakativ – mit einem Wort von Alvar Aalto aus dem Jahr 1938 – vor dem »winzigen Menschen« und machen ihn wieder groß: »Im Unterschied zu der Auffassung, die in den etablierten Formen und in der Standardisierung neuer Formen den einzigen Weg zu einer architektonischen Harmonie und zu einer Bautechnik, die erfolgreich kontrolliert werden kann, sieht ..., will ich unterstreichen, daß die weitgehendste Eigenart der Architektur eine Variante und eine Erinnerung an das Wachstum des natürlichen organischen Lebens ist. Ich möchte sagen, dass dies letzten Endes der einzige wirklich architektonische Stil ist. Wenn dem Schranken gesetzt werden, verblüht und stirbt die Architektur.« Die Botschaften der Nordischen Länder sind der Beleg dafür: »Intuition kann manchmal unerhört rational sein.« Unwillkürlich stellt sich so der Verdacht ein, es könnte – völlig anders, aber doch verwandt – eine unverhoffte Fortschreibung des Werkes von Alvar Aalto geben.

Geschichte und Typologie der Botschaftsgebäude werden von nun an in zwei Epochen – vor und nach den Botschaften der Nordischen Länder – zu behandeln sein. Wollte man die Ideengeschichte der in Berlin realisierten urbanen Metasprache zurückverfolgen, würde man ein weiteres Mal auf Alvar Aalto stoßen. In den frühen fünfziger Jahren äußerte sich der Architekt – der Stützen in lackierte Blechmäntel hüllte und Fassaden in mosaikartigen Backstein, strahlenden Marmor, leuchtende Kacheln oder schimmernden Schiefer – über die Dekadenz der städtischen Bauten und beklagte, daß die architektonischen Leistungen des Staates überschattet würden. Sein Rat damals, um ein Gegengewicht zur Boomtown der Büropaläste und Industriebauten zu schaffen: Konzentration mehrerer staatlicher Einrichtungen zu größeren Komplexen.

Die Architektur von Berger + Parkkinen wagt sinnreiche Grenzgänge, nicht nur zwischen den beteiligten Ländern, sondern auch zwischen Städtebau und Architektur, Technik und Kunst. In den Botschaftskomplex ist der Stadtraum ebenso integriert wie die Natur. Materialien und Möbel zeigen unterschiedliche Kulturen: eine kleine, aber dafür auf Dauer angelegte »Weltausstellung« der nordischen Länder, die dank der umspannenden Land Art, für die das gewählte Material Kupfer kaum geeigneter sein könnte, nicht in einzelne Pavillons auseinanderfällt. Bei aller Offenheit und Transparenz, die in der Dunkelheit zu einem Schauspiel wird, in dem das textile Eingangsdach, die weißen Marmorfugen, die Wasserflächen der Plaza leuchten und das Kupferband im Streiflicht strahlt, lebt die Komposition von überaus exakten, perspektivisch verstärkten Raumfolgen und präzisen, gleichhohen Gebäudekanten, die das zunächst abstrakte, amorphe Volumen, das im Verhältnis zum Tiergarten einen Maßstabssprung realisiert, im Inneren in Spannung versetzen. Faszinierend zu sehen, wie der neutralisierte Raum des Gitters, das rigide Raster Manhattans oder das "X" als altägyptische Hieroglyphe für Stadt innerhalb der organisch fließenden Kupferbegrenzung dieses Bauwerks, das eine Stadt ist, zu dynamischen Variationen findet.

Bemerkenswert ist, wie dieses Ziel architektonisch und organisatorisch erreicht worden ist. Denn die federführenden Architekten des Gesamtkonzepts ließen den Architekten der Botschaften ungewöhnlich viel Spielraum. Nicht einmal die Tiefgarage mit 88 Einstellplätzen wurde in ihren konstruktiven Eckdaten vorgegeben. Das führte zwar zu einem enormen Planungsaufwand im Büro Berger + Parkkinen, aber, abgesehen von der allein verbindlichen Kubatur, auch zur totalen Entwurfsfreiheit der beteiligten Architekten. Ebenso wenig mußten sich die Architekten der einzelnen Botschaften einem vorgegebenem Öffnungsraster des Kupferbands beugen. Dieser Abschluß entstand vielmehr als autogenerierte Fassade im nachhinein, auf der Basis fertiger Gebäudeentwürfe. Auch in diesem Punkt arbeiteten Alfred Berger und Tiina Parkkinen mithin grenzüberschreitend.

Die nordischen Länder, insbesondere das mit fünf Millionen Einwohnern nicht gerade mächtige Finnland, führen uns vor, wie Baukultur zu einer politischen Größe werden kann.[9] In Finnland existiert seit dem hundertsten Geburtstag Alvar Aaltos, dem 17. Dezember 1998, eine regierungsamtliche Architekturpolitik mit nicht weniger als 24 Programmpunkten. Nach zweijähriger öffentlicher Diskussion, nach der Beratung in zwei Kommissionen, in denen auch, aber nicht nur Architekten vertreten waren, ist die Initiative des Erziehungsministeriums in die Tat umgesetzt worden. Hiernach haben die Bürger Finnlands einen gesetzlich zugesicherten Anspruch auf eine sorgsam gestaltete Umwelt vom Einzelgebäude bis hin zur Landschaftsgestaltung und zum Straßenbau – getreu der Forderung Vitruvs, daß die Dinge dauerhaft, nützlich und anmutig zu sein hätten.

[1] Vgl. Klaus-Dieter Weiß (Hrsg.), *Bernhard Winking: Architektur und Stadt / Architecture and the City*, Basel, Boston und Berlin 1999, S. 132 f.

[2] »Berlin's new parliament«, *The Guardian*, 20.4.1999.

[3] Edward Pearce, »Capital gains and losses«, *The Guardian*, 26.6.1991.

[4] Jonathan Glancey, »The eagle has risen«, *The Guardian*, 19.4.1999.

[5] Peter Davey, »Dissecting the diplomatic«, *The Architectural Review*, 3/2000, S. 38 f.

[5] Jonathan Glancey, »In the midst of a building blitz«, *The Independent*, 24.11.1993.

[7] Vgl. Ingeborg Flagge und Wolfgang Jean Stock, *Architektur und Demokratie*, Stuttgart 1996 (1992), S. 70.

[8] Vgl. Rudolf Maresch, »Vorhöfe der Macht«, *Telepolis*, 13.1.2000.

[9] Vgl. Gert Kähler, »Wo die Häuser leuchten«, *Frankfurter Allgemeine Zeitung*, 2.2.2000.

dic Countries. In Berlin, the copper band, in its material quality and energetic dynamic, embodies the nature component, or the counter-image of reality. And there is something that one does not suspect at first: even the regular order of the copper slats is broken in the curvature of the building. The width of the elements fluctuates in five sizes between 90 and 180 cm, dependent on the curvature at a particular moment.

This motif is involuntarily reminiscent of Finnish lake landscapes, which have already inspired Alvar Aalto to produce soft, curving and organic forms: for the first time in 1930, for the undulating ceiling in the lecture hall of the library in Viipuri, and later for vases, door-handles, lamps, furniture and room-dividers that were mobile in three dimensions. This is an image that recurs in the interior of the Danish Embassy and the »cloud« floating in the atrium that is in fact the Finnish conference room. This is an image intended to defy the danger of excessive rationalization, the threat from political, technical and economic planning that sacrifices deep-rooted cultural and sensual values in the search for easily achieved aims. This is the reason for the enormously positive response to the Embassies of the Nordic Countries from Berlin itself, but also from all over the world. The mysterious, unaccountable façade, broken in a thousand pieces, nowhere identical in its colour details arising from natural forces, and yet still »green«, drawing back from the old and the new stock of trees to make the individual embassies into a single whole, is a record of a philosophy, not a building. The image of the sterile city, dominating individuals, gives way to something that symbolizes the self-perception of the Nordic countries, which are far more closely connected than is generally known.

Here the claim to power that political architecture usually likes to stake collides visibly here with a long democratic tradition, with the aim for equal rights, with the place value of nature and environment, with representing the rights of nature and the rights of man. Thus the Embassies of the Nordic Countries are a bold and simple warning – to quote Alvar Aalto in 1938 – against »tiny man«, and give him back his stature: »in contrast with the view that sees the only way to architectural harmony and to building technology that can be successfully controlled in established forms and the standardization of new forms ... I should like to emphasize that architecture's most far-reaching quality is a variant and memory of the growth of natural organic life. I would like to say that ultimately this is the only aim of architecture. If barriers are placed in the way of this, architecture will fade and die.« The Embassies of the Nordic Countries are proof of this: »Intuition can sometimes be enormously rational.« Sometimes one cannot help sensing that Alvar Aalto's architecture could be continued unexpectedly – in a way that is completely different, but related.

The history and typology of embassy buildings will from now on have to be treated in two epochs – before and after the Embassies of the Nordic Countries. If one wanted to trace back the history of ideas that lies behind the urban meta-language realized in Berlin, one would once more come across Alvar Aalto. In the early fifties, the architect – who was covering columns in painted sheet-metal, and façades in mosaic-like brick, glowing marble, gleaming tiles or shimmering slate – spoke about the decadence of municipal buildings and complained that they were overshadowing the archi-

tectural achievements of the state. The advice he gave at the time, in order to create a counterweight to the boom-town of the offices palaces and industrial buildings: that several state institutions should be concentrated in large complexes.

Berger + Parkkinen's architecture dares to cross borders in a profoundly significant way, and these are not just borders between the countries involved, but also between urban development and architecture, technology and art. Urban space is integrated into the embassy complex to just as great an extent as nature. Materials and furniture indicate different cultures: this is a small but permanent »world fair« of the Nordic countries, which, thanks to the Land Art that surrounds it, for which the chosen material, copper, could hardly be more suitable, does not fall apart into individual pavilions. Despite all its openness and transparency – qualities that become a drama after dark in which the textile entrance canopy, the white marble joints, the surfaces of the water in the plaza glow and the copper band gleams where highlighted, the composition draws its life from extremely exact spatial sequences, reinforced by perspective, and precise edges of buildings placed at equal heights that set the initial abstract, amorphous volume, which achieves a break of scale in relationship with the Tiergarten, in a state of tension in the interior. It is fascinating to see how the neutralized space of the grid, Manhattan's rigid pattern or the X as an ancient Egyptian hieroglyph for city, finds its way to dynamic variations within the organically fluent copper border of this building, which is a city.

It is remarkable how this aim has been achieved architecturally and in terms of organization. The architects who were in control of the project as a whole gave the embassy architects an enormous amount of room for manœuvre. Not even the underground car-park with its 88 spaces was laid down in constructive detail. This certainly led to a great deal of planning effort in Berger + Parkkinen's office but, apart from the cubic content, which was the only binding element, to total design freedom for the architects involved. And the architects of the individual embassies did not have to submit to a prescribed opening grid for the copper band either. This conclusion to the building as a whole in fact emerged retrospectively, on the basis of complete building designs. Thus Alfred Berger and Tiina Parkkinen were working across boundaries in this respect as well.

The Nordic countries, especially Finland, whose five million inhabitants do not exactly make it powerful, showed us how building culture can become a political quantity.[9] Since Alvar Aalto's hundredth birthday, 17 December 1998, Finland has had an official government architecture policy with no fewer than 24 points on its programme. After two years of public discussion, after consultations in two commissions, including architects, but not just architects, the Education Ministry's initiative became reality. It means that the people of Finland have a legal right to a carefully designed environment, from the individual building right down to landscape design and road construction – in keeping with the Vitruvian requirements for things to be useful, solid and beautiful.

[1] Cf. Klaus-Dieter Weiß (ed.), *Bernhard Winking: Architektur und Stadt / Architecture and the City*, Basel, Boston and Berlin, 1999, pp. 132 f.
[2] »Berlin's new parliament«, *The Guardian*, 20 April 1999.
[3] Edward Pierce, »Capital gains and losses«, *The Guardian*, 26 June 1991.
[4] Jonathan Glancey, »The eagle has risen«, *The Guardian*, 19 April 1999.
[5] Peter Davey, »Dissecting the diplomatic«, *The Architectural Review*, 3/2000, pp. 38 f.
[5] Jonathan Glancey, »In the midst of a building blitz«, *The Independent*, 24 November 1993.
[7] Cf. Ingeborg Flagge and Wolfgang Jean Stock, *Architektur und Demokratie*, Stuttgart, 1996 (1992), p. 70.
[8] Cf. Rudolf Maresch, »Vorhöfe der Macht«, *Telepolis*, 13 January 2000.
[9] Cf. Gert Kähler, »Wo die Häuser leuchten«, *Frankfurter Allgemeine Zeitung*, 2 February 2000.

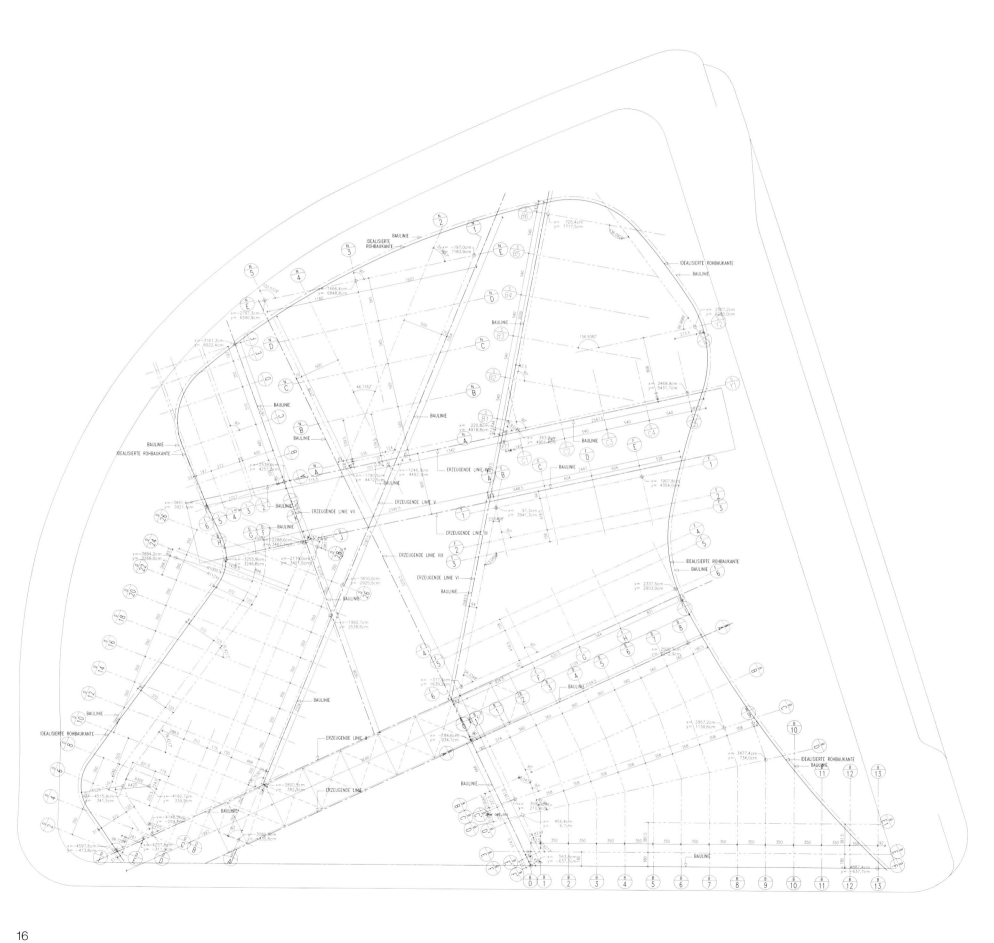

16

1. Achsenplan.
2. Lageplan. 1 Gemeinschaftshaus, 2 Finnland, 3 Schwe-
den, 4 Norwegen, 5 Island, 6 Dänemark.

1. Axis plan.
2. Site plan. 1 communal building, 2 Finland, 3 Swe-
den, 4 Norway, 5 Iceland, 6 Denmark.

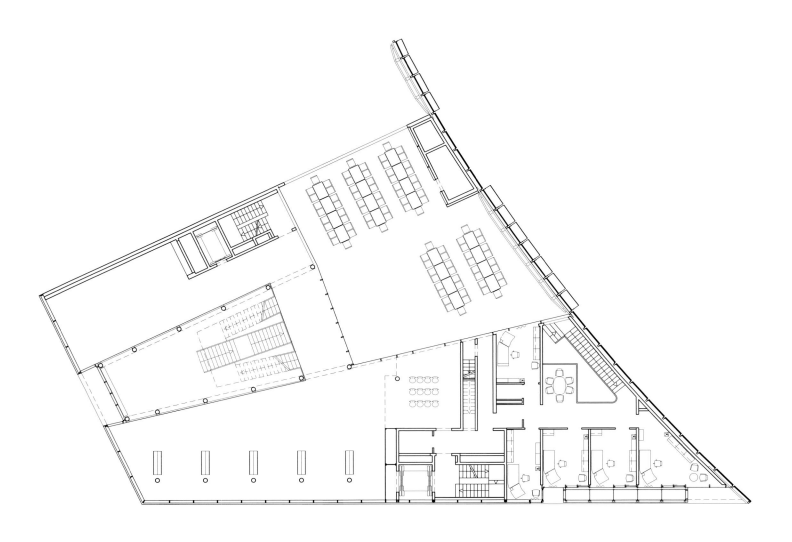

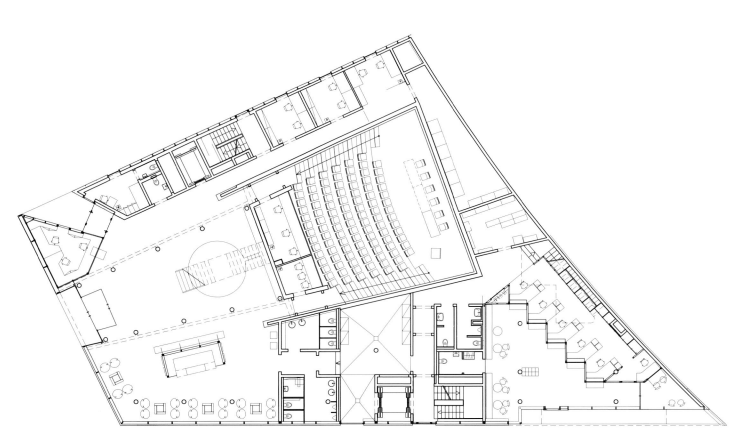

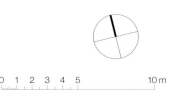

0 1 2 3 4 5   10 m

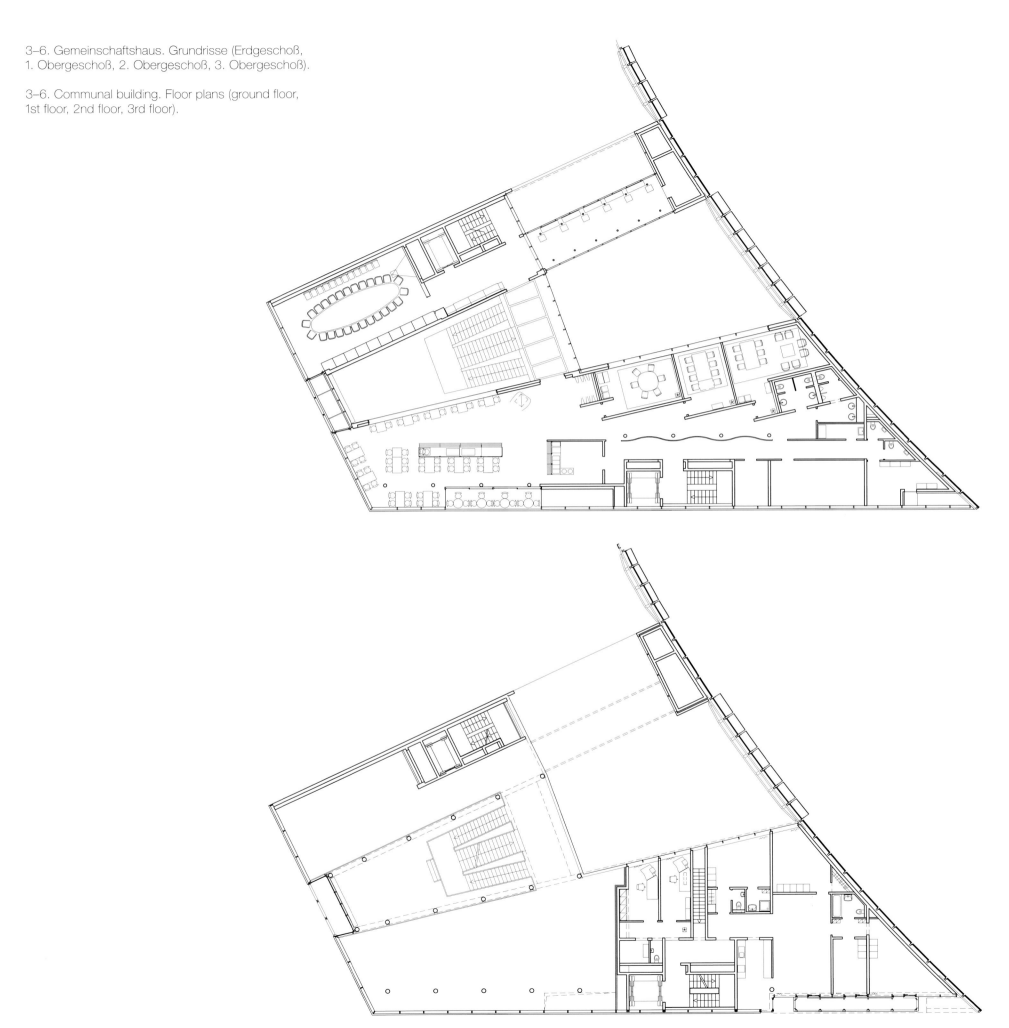

3–6. Gemeinschaftshaus. Grundrisse (Erdgeschoß,
1. Obergeschoß, 2. Obergeschoß, 3. Obergeschoß).

3–6. Communal building. Floor plans (ground floor,
1st floor, 2nd floor, 3rd floor).

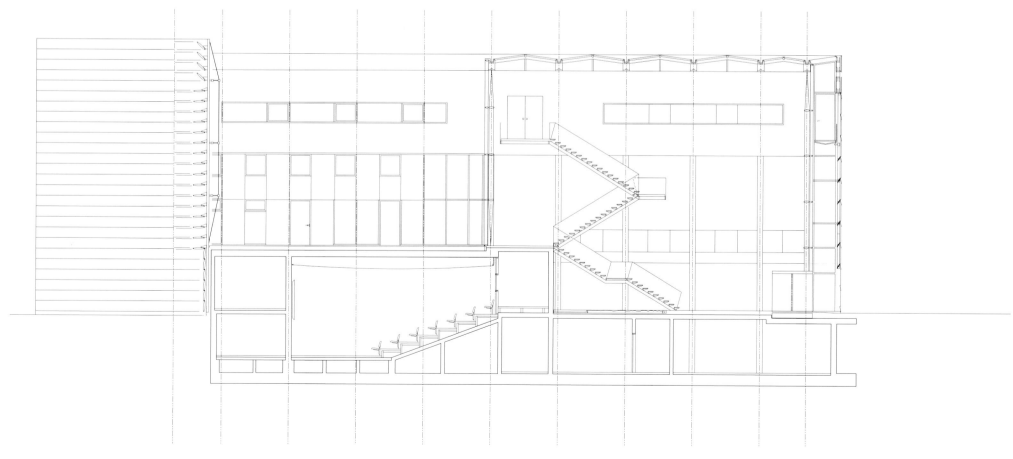

7. Gemeinschaftshaus. Schnitt.
8. Gemeinschaftshaus. Aufriß der Südseite.

7. Communal building. Section.
8. Communal building. Elevation of the south side.

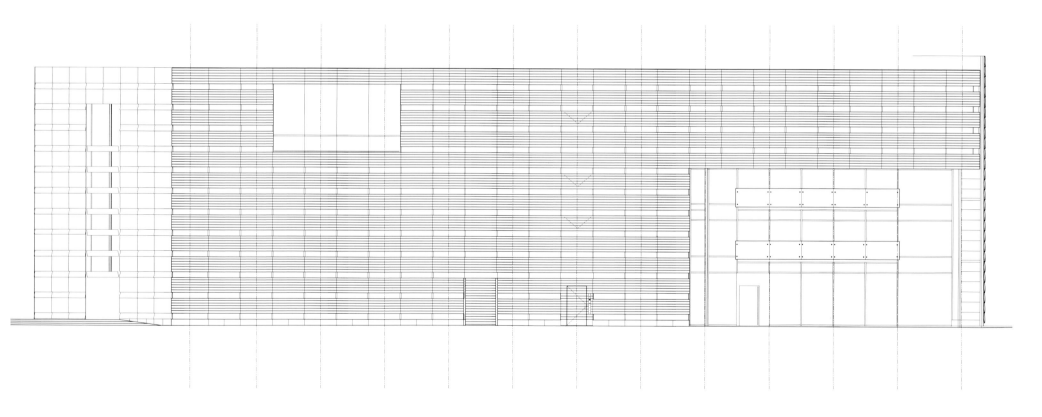

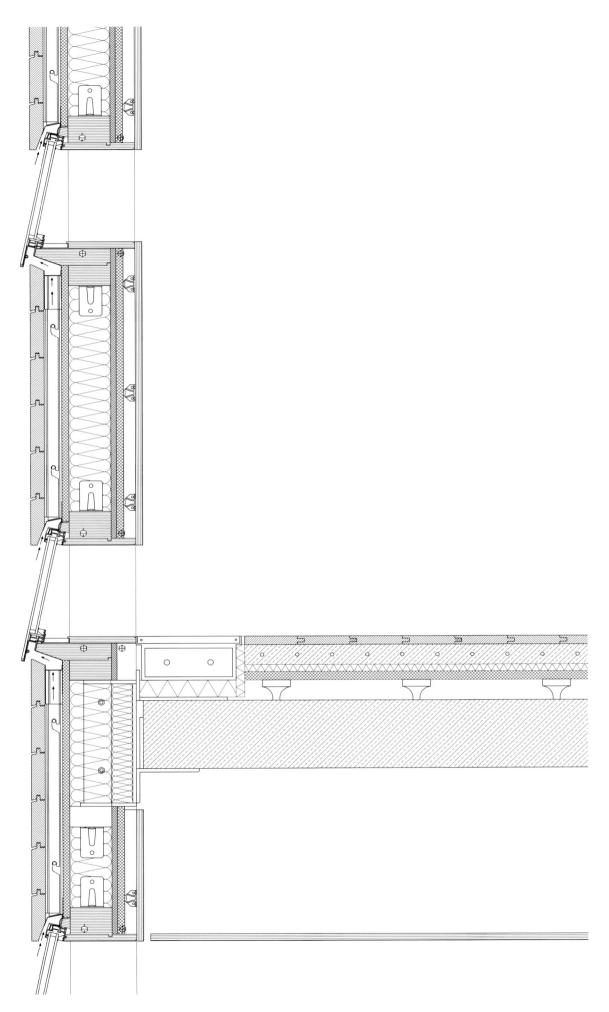

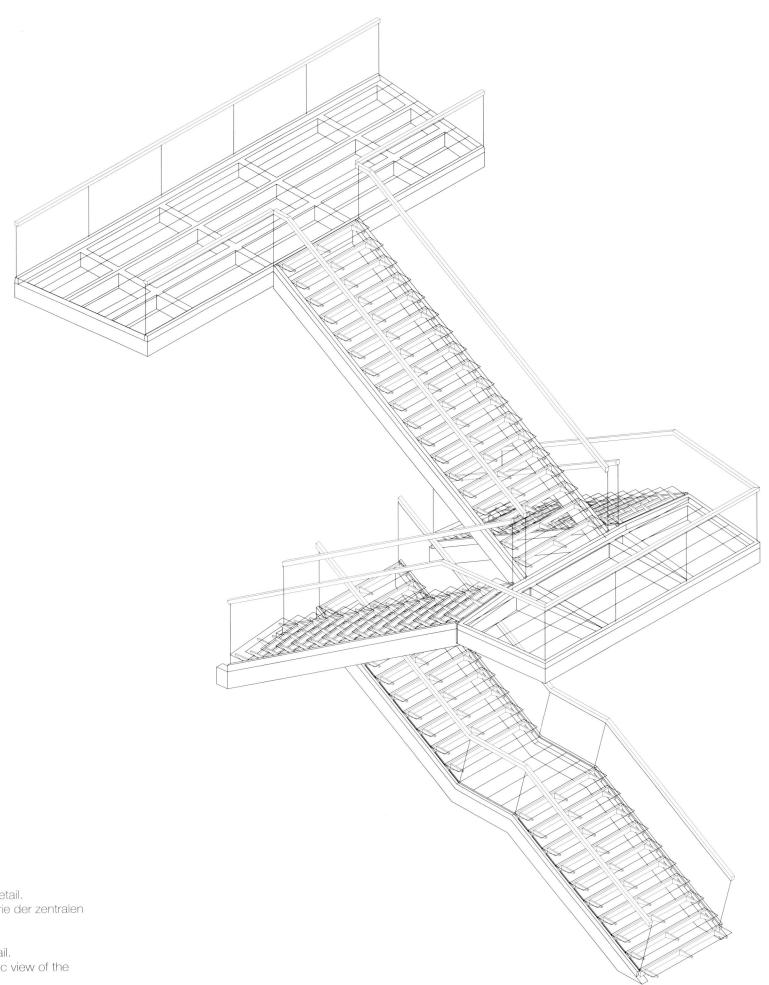

9. Gemeinschaftshaus. Fassadendetail.
10. Gemeinschaftshaus. Axonometrie der zentralen
Treppenanlage.

9. Communal building. Façade detail.
10. Communal building. Axonometric view of the
central staircase.

11. Axonometrie des Kupferbands.
12. Detail des Kupferbands.

11. Axonometric view of the copper band.
12. Detail of the copper band.

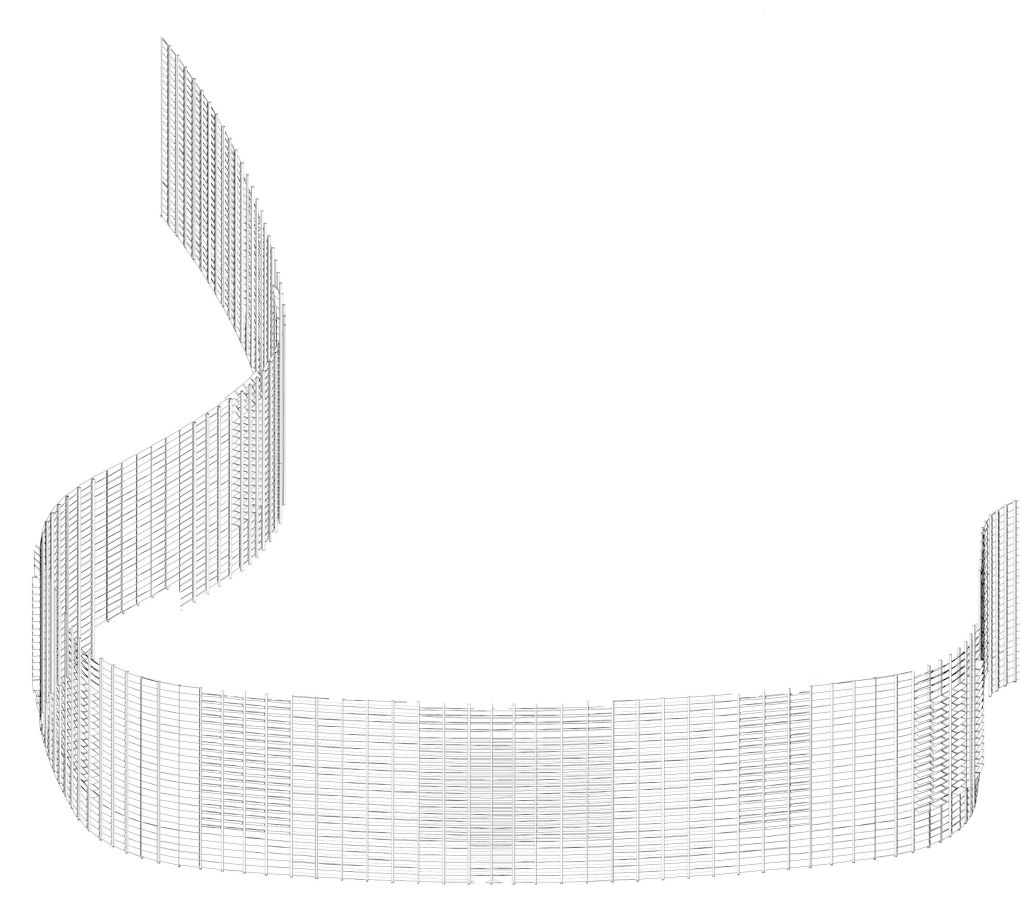

24

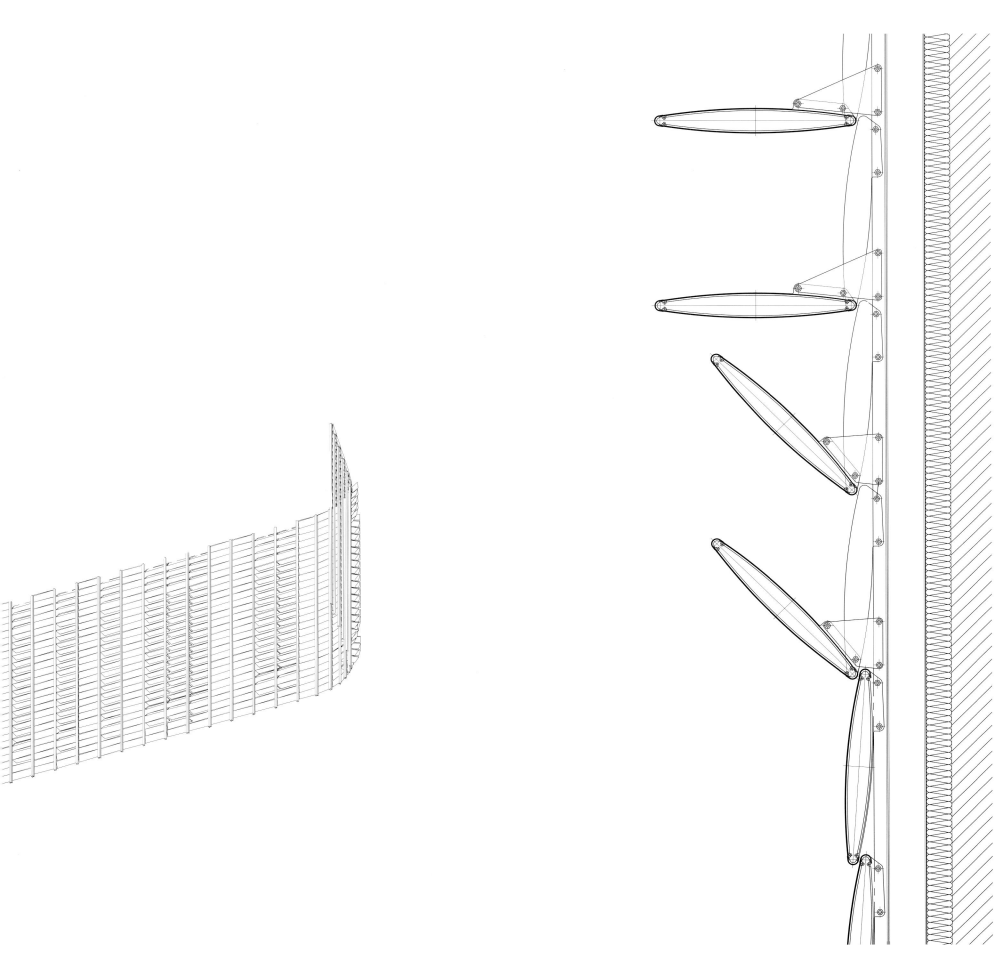

6. Die Südostecke des Komplexes. Links die Rauchstraße, rechts die Klingelhöferstraße.
7, 8. Blick von der Rauchstraße auf den Komplex.
Links die Dänische Botschaft, rechts das Gemeinschaftshaus.

6. The south-east corner of the complex. Rauchstraße
on the left, Klingelhöferstraße on the right.
7, 8. View of the complex from Rauchstraße. The
Danish Embassy on the left, the communal building
on the right.

S. 34/35
9. Die Eingangsseite des Gemeinschaftshauses.

p. 34/35
9. The entrance side of the communal building.

S. 36, 37
10, 11. Die zentrale Treppenanlage im Gemeinschafts-haus.

p. 36, 37
10, 11. The central staircase in the communal building.

12. Die Nebentreppe an der Nordseite des Gemeinschaftshauses.
13. Die Nebentreppe an der Ostseite des Gemeinschaftshauses.

12. The secondary staircase on the north side of the
communal building.
13. The secondary staircase on the east side of the
communal building.

14. Der Konsularbereich in der Südostecke des Gemeinschaftshauses.

14. The consular area in the south-east corner of the communal building.

Suomen Suurlähetystö -Konsulaatidien osasto
Finlands Ambassad -Konsulära Avdelningen
Botschaft von Finnland

Sveriges Ambassad -Konsulära Avdelningen
Schwedische Botschaft

S. 42/43
15. Das Auditorium im Gemeinschaftshaus.

p. 42/43
15. The auditorium in the communal building.

16, 17. Der Ausstellungsbereich im 1. und 2. Obergeschoß des Gemeinschaftshauses.

16, 17. The exhibition area on the 1st and 2nd floors of the communal building.

18. Vorraum des Sitzungssaales im 3. Obergeschoß des Gemeinschaftshauses.
19. Der Sitzungssaal im 3. Obergeschoß des Gemeinschaftshauses.

18. Anteroom of the conference room on the 3rd floor of the communal building.
19. The conference room on the 3rd floor of the communal building.

20, 21. Der Dachgarten im 2. Obergeschoß des Gemeinschaftshauses. Im Hintergrund die Finnische Botschaft.

20, 21. The roof garden on the 2nd floor of the communal
building. In the background the Finnish Embassy.

S. 50/51
22. Links das Gemeinschaftshaus, rechts die Finnische
Botschaft. Im Hintergrund rechts die Dänische Botschaft.

p. 50/51
22. The communal building on the left, the Finnish Embassy on the right. In the background right the Danish
Embassy.

S. 54, 55

23. Links die Norwegische, in der Mitte die Schwedische, rechts die Finnische Botschaft.
24. Links die Norwegische, rechts die Schwedische und die Finnische Botschaft.

S. 54, 55
25. Die Isländische Botschaft.
26. Links die Finnische, rechts die Isländische Botschaft.

23. The Norwegian Embassy on the left, the Swedish Embassy in the centre, the Finnish Embassy on the right.
24. The Norwegian Embassy on the left, the Swedish and the Finnish Embassies on the right.

p. 54, 55
25. The Icelandic Embassy.
26. The Finnish Embassy on the left, the Icelandic Embassy on the right.

27. Links die Dänische und die Isländische Botschaft, in der Mitte die Norwegische Botschaft, rechts die Schwedische Botschaft und das Gemeinschaftshaus.
28. Links die Schwedische Botschaft, rechts die Finnische Botschaft.

27. The Danish and the Icelandic Embassies on the left, the Norwegian Embassy in the centre, the Swedish Embassy and the communal building on the right.
28. The Swedish Embassy on the left, the Finnish Embassy on the right.

S. 58/59
29. Links die Norwegische Botschaft, rechts die Schwedische und die Finnische Botschaft.

p. 58/59
29. The Norwegian Embassy on the left, the Swedish and the Finnish Embassies on the right.

Die Botschaften der Nordischen Länder
Rauchstraße 1
10787 Berlin

Architekten/Architects
Gesamtanlage/General design Berger + Parkkinen
Architekten (Alfred Berger, Tiina Parkkinen), Wien/
Vienna
*Gemeinschaftshaus, Tiefgeschoß, Kupferband, Au-
ßenanlagen/Communal building, basement, copper
band, exterior equipment* Berger + Parkkinen Architek-
ten (Alfred Berger, Tiina Parkkinen), Wien/Vienna; Mit-
arbeiter/collaborators: Margarete Dietrich, Antti Laiho,
Ines Nicic, Thomas Pirker, Kurt Sattler, Peter Thalbauer,
Günther Unterfrauner, Ivan Zdenkovic
Dänische Botschaft/Danish Embassy Nielsen, Niel-
sen & Nielsen AS (Lars Frank Nielsen, Kim Herforth Nielsen), Århus; Mitarbeiter/collaborators: Gerti Axelsen,
Lars Kjemtrup, Lars Due Jensen, Helge Skovsted, Jette
Schwarz, Lars Povlsen, Mads Posch, Malene E. Knud-
sen, Jørgen Søndermark, Svend Blichfeldt
Finnische Botschaft/Finnish Embassy VIIVA arkkiteh-
tuuri Oy (Rauno Lehtinen, Pekka Mäki, Toni Peltola), Hel-
sinki
Isländische Botschaft/Icelandic Embassy Pálmar
Kristmundsson, Reykjavik; Wettbewerbsentwurf/com-
petition design: Pálmar Kristmundsson, Gunnar Berg-
mann Stefánsson; Projektplanung/project planning: Pál-
mar Kristmundsson, Birgir Teitsson, Haraldur Ingvarsson,
Sindri Gunnarsson
Norwegische Botschaft/Norwegian Embassy Snøhet-
ta as (Craig Dykers, Christoph Kapeller, Kjetil T. Thor-
sen), Oslo; Wettbewerbsentwurf/competition design:
Craig Dykers, Christoph Kapeller, Kjetil T. Thorsen; Pro-
jektplanung/project planning: Jostein Bjørndahl, Ibrahim
El-Hayawan, Ole Gustavsen, Frank Kristiansen, Knut
Tronstad; Landschaftsarchitektin/Landscape architect:
Ragnhild Momrak
Schwedische Botschaft/Swedish Embassy Wingårdh
Arkitektkontor AB (Gert Wingårdh), Göteborg; Wettbe-
werbsentwurf/competition design: Per Glembrandt, Ul-
rika Bergström, Vanja Knocke, Thomas Ocklund, Jerry
Kopare, Pal Ericksson, Fredrick Gullberg, Anneli Carls-
son; Projektplanung/project planning: Torbjörn Edgren,
Gunilla Murnieks, Dan Danielsson, Björn Dufva, Johan
Casselbrant, Smajo Stender, Anna Evaldsson, Jonny
Dernbrant, Erik Williamsson; Inneneinrichtung/interior
design: Gert Wingårdh, Solweig Sörman. Büroausstat-
tung/Office equipment: White Arkitekter, Elisabeth Ro-
senlund

Projektmanagement/Project management
Drees & Sommer AG, Berlin

Kontaktarchitekten und Bauleitung/Local archi-
tects and site management
Pysall u. Ruge Architekten, Berlin; Mitarbeiter/collabo-
rators: Bettina Menzel, Gerhard Papenburg, Thomas
Arnold, Kathrin Bunte, James Geiger, Michaela Kunze,
Rolf Leinweber, Axel Meißner, Luyanda Mpahlwa

Tragwerksplanung/Structural engineering
IGH Ingenieurgesellschaft Höpfner mbH, Berlin

Haustechnik/Mechanical engineering
IGH Ingenieurgesellschaft Höpfner mbH, Köln/Cologne

Fassadentechnik für das Kupferband und das
Gemeinschaftshaus/Façade engineering for the
copper band and the communal building
DEWI Ingenieurbüro GmbH, Wien/Vienna

Bauphysik und Fassadentechnik für die ein-
zelnen Botschaften/Structural physics and
façade engineering for the individual embassies
DS-Plan Ingenieurgesellschaft für ganzheitliche Bau-
beratung u. -planung, Stuttgart

Lichtplanung/Lighting design
George Sexton Associates, Washington, DC

Grünplanung/Landscape design
Karsten Böcking, Hannover

Bodengutachten/Soil analysis
GuD – Geotechnik und Dynamik Consult GmbH,
Berlin

Brandschutz/Fire prevention
Hosser, Hass + Partner GmbH, Berlin

Die folgenden am Bau der Anlage beteiligten Firmen
haben die Herausgabe dieses Buches finanziell unter-
stützt:
The following firms involved in the construction of the
complex have given financial support to the publication
of this book:

August Pattberg Schreinerei Möbel, Bocholt
DEWI Ingenieurbüro GmbH, Wien/Vienna
Drees & Sommer AG, Berlin
DS-Plan Ingenieurgesellschaft für ganzheitliche Bau-
    beratung u. -planung, Stuttgart
elkosta GmbH, Grundstückssicherungen, Salzgitter
Epping Metallbau GmbH & Co. KG, Bocholt
Franz Bamberger Gesellschaft mbH, Traiskirchen
Gebr. Kufferath GmbH & Co. KG, Düren
GuD – Geotechnik und Dynamik Consult GmbH, Berlin
Hark GmbH & Co. KG, Herford
Holzbau Seufert-Niklaus GmbH, Bastheim
Hosser, Hass + Partner GmbH, Berlin
Ing. A. Sauritschnig Alu-Stahl-Glas-Gesellschaft m. b. H.,
    St. Veit/Glan
IGH Ingenieurgesellschaft Höpfner mbH, Köln/Cologne
KM Europa Metal AG, Osnabrück
Kurt Boecker Büro- und Raumgestaltung GmbH, Berlin
Krantz-TKT GmbH, Bergisch Gladbach
Leonhard Weiss GmbH & Co., Crailsheim
Rheiner Stahlbau GmbH, Georgsmarienhütte